A DARK VIEW FROM THE TOWER

PRISON BARZ AND POETIC WARZ

ALSHAUN DIXON

A Dark View From The Tower
Copyright © 2021 by Alshaun Dixon

All rights reserved. No part of this publication may be reproduced, distributed, or transmitted in any form or by any means, including photocopying, recording, or other electronic or mechanical methods, without the prior written permission of the author, except in the case of brief quotations embodied in critical reviews and certain other non-commercial uses permitted by copyright law.

Tellwell Talent
www.tellwell.ca

ISBN
978-0-2288-6109-6 (Hardcover)
978-0-2288-6108-9 (Paperback)

DEDICATION

To my father, Alexander "Pete" Dixon, for empowering me with a strong sense of Black pride and a desire to celebrate Black culture and embrace my African heritage.

CONTENTS

Preface vii
Introduction x
Prologue xiii

PART I
PRISON LIFE

1. Exposing the Cracks 2
2. Chasing Cheese 4
3. Hit the Gate 6
4. Walk the Line 8
5. Tuff Luv 12
6. Busted on the Block 15
7. Lockdown 17
8. Slide a Neega a Burrito 18
9. Puttin' the Smack Down 20
10. Is Real 21
11. E-O Muthafuggin P 22
12. Can I Get a Crack 24
13. I'm a Porter 25
14. Hittin' the Cell 27
15. Beggin' a Bitch 29
16. Gettin' It In 33
17. Passin' Out Condoms 37
18. Green Fish 39
19. Bump and Mump 41
20. Blackballed 42
21. Toy Soldiers 46
22. Fake Ass Sarjent 48

23. Poison Coolaide 50
24. Snitchin 'N' Bitchin 52
25. Chillin' on the Honor Yard 54

PART II
STRUGGLE 'N' STRIFE

26. The Black Crack Attack 60
27. Batter Ram 63
28. Son Down 66
29. Set Trippin' 67
30. Chicken Hennessee Weed 68
31. Neegaritis 71
32. No Mo Ass Kissin' 74
33. The March of Crimes 76
34. Hear the Cries 78
35. Neegas Crakkas and Wedbacks 81
36. Black Lives Madder 85
37. The New Civil War 86
38. Unite the Fight 88
39. Kappa Nigg 90
40. A Ball of Flames 93
41. RIP Nip the Crip 96
42. I Can't Breathe 100
43. Sell Me a River 103
44. Pimpin' in the Pulpit 105
45. Field Service 109
46. Jus Got Paid 111
47. Fire Impire 112
48. Crackatosis Hypnosis 114
49. Stop Black Destruction 117
50. Wake Up, My Brotha 119

PREFACE

The lights were dim and the house quiet as the floor officers walked down the tier, completing the sixteen hundred count. I sat down and opened my bag for a bite to eat. I grabbed a pen and pad and began to write my first poem, describing prison life from my dark viewpoint in the tower.

I was employed for eighteen years with the State of California and worked as a Correctional Officer for the Department of Corrections in Los Angeles County. I have worked several positions inside this penitentiary, including housing units, dormitories, chow halls, and administrative segregation/Ad Seg units. Ad Seg is often referred to as the "HOLE." These units are usually reserved for those who commit the more horrific crimes while incarcerated and for prisoners who are a serious danger to themselves or others. I've also escorted inmates, attorneys, and judges for interviews and board hearings. I've driven inmates to medical appointments and provided security while the inmate was handcuffed to his hospital bed. I've also worked on the yard, responding to alarms in freezing winters and blazing hot summers. I've worked in the watch office, central control, visiting, the main gate, and suicide watches.

But the position I preferred the most was situated inside the control booth, also known as the tower. It's an armed post. I provided protection, safety, and security from an elevated booth approximately twenty feet high located in the middle of the housing unit. The control booth officer runs the whole show by utilizing an electronic panel to open and close all cell doors for inmates. The officer passes out all equipment for housing unit officers and communicates with custody staff members and medical personnel when they enter the building. Duties include directing inmate traffic, answering phone calls, keeping daily logs, and providing reports on inmate violations while keeping close tabs on all inmate movement. Round the clock multitasking is the reason why the control booth is one of the most disliked positions in the joint. This assignment allowed me to work in a space alone and away from the unprofessionalism within the department. The racist jokes, unnecessary force, sexist comments, cliques, politics, favoritism, bragging, intimidation, manipulation, humiliation, flirtation, assumption, corruption, and gossip were all part of a typical day with my co-workers. I got tired of dealing with the continuous pissing contest and decided it would be in my best interest to distance myself from the shenanigans. I needed a post that would allow me to be firm, fair, and consistent at all times.

    Careful movement is required when swimming in shark infested waters. Keeping your head on a swivel can protect you from being swallowed into the belly of the beast. Of course, the control booth post had its daily challenges with staff and inmates as well, but I felt it was the best place for me to be the most effective. I wasn't hiding behind a badge or positional rank, like some of my partners. I had personal power. I'm not talking about physicality. The guy with the biggest muscles is not winning the fight in his arena. This is a mental game of chess. The object of the game is for the white king to checkmate the black king. White is always on offense and makes the first move. The black king is under immediate attack and is in a defensive position. Yes, this is the plight of all Black men. It doesn't matter if you're rich or poor, educated or illiterate, well dressed or unkept, officer or an inmate. You are under constant pressure.

I was always true to myself. I had a figurative master's degree from the school of hard knocks. I grew up in an area referred to as the "low bottoms" of South Central Los Angeles, California. Beginning in the late 1970s, the neighborhood began to experience a rise in drug related crimes and gang activity, and many young men were incarcerated because of these circumstances. I studied behaviors in this human zoo, and I communicated well with people from various backgrounds. My verbal skills and discernment were second to none. I related well with the downtrodden. I always said a prayer and checked my personal feelings at the gate. My goal was to shine a little light within the darkness and bring a spirit of peace amidst the war.

Whenever I had a break from work, I would write down a few thoughts and create a poem depicting prison life and the conditions within the struggle and strife. I also added social commentary addressing the systemic racism that led the push for mass incarceration. I sprinkled in some much-needed humor to enhance the flavor of this boiling mixture of hope and despair. These poems are full of Ebonics, urban slang, broken English, and satire. They are influenced by my interactions and conversations with inmates and staff, and by personal observations. The cadence, the flow, and the bars reflect my love for hip hop, the rhyme and poetic lyricists. This is my dark view from the tower.

INTRODUCTION

It was 1969. My father was unemployed, and his Doo Wop music era was over. Martin Luther King Jr. had been assassinated the year before. South Central Los Angeles was still smoldering from the Watts Riot, and James Brown sang, "Say it loud, I'm Black and I'm proud." My dad was a proud Black man, but he was frustrated and bitter with his status in an unjust world. One day he ripped out a dollar food stamp from the booklet and sent me to the corner store to get a loaf of bread. Mr. Wong, the store owner, wouldn't accept the slightly torn and loose food stamp and rudely told me to get out of his store. I was only five years old. I was the oldest of three kids at home, and my parents trusted me to handle the responsibility. Tears welled up in my eyes as I walked back home to tell my dad that Mr. Wong wouldn't let me buy the bread. I was disappointed because I really wanted that bread for my peanut butter and jelly sandwich for lunch.

My dad was drinking a can of malt liquor and became angry and immediately headed to the store to confront Wong for disrespecting his son. An argument ensued, and my father's temper began to rise. He proceeded to knock the pickled pig feet jar, the boxes of candy bars, and moon pies off the store counter onto the floor. The police were called and arrived quickly. They handcuffed my dad and beat him up. He was shoved into the back seat of the police car, and they took him to jail. He returned home a few days later with a badly bruised face and stitches in his head. It was hurtful and traumatic to see my dad get beaten and bloodied for trying to defend me. This was my introduction to police brutality.

Power to the people. The Black Panthers were heroes in my community— not the police. The number one enemy of Black people was the "Pig." I developed a long-lasting hatred for everything connected to law enforcement. My Black power fist was raised high in the air.

Now fast forward over thirty years later. Imagine the look on my father's face when I finally got enough nerve to tell him that I was about to work in a prison as a correctional officer. He couldn't believe it. He was shocked. He took a long draw on his cigarette, exhaled, and with a confused look asked, "What? Why are you doing that shit?" I began to explain to him how difficult it was for me to get promoted at my current job. I was an intelligent Black man and had all of the credentials to qualify for the position. I ranked high on the test and interviews, but I'd get passed over for the promotion. It was my obligation to provide for my family, and this new career afforded me that opportunity. Initially, he didn't like my decision, but he understood it and respected the fact that I was mature and responsible enough to handle the situation. He looked me in my eyes and uttered these words: "Watch your back, and don't let nobody fuck with you!" Those words stayed with me as I began to walk the "toughest beat in the state."

It was never my dream to wear a badge, boots, and a uniform. I had never been inside of a jail or prison. I didn't know the difference between a sergeant, lieutenant, or captain. Even though I graduated from the Correctional Officer Academy, it still felt weird to be called an officer, a cop, or a prison guard. I often asked myself, "Am I really doing this? What have I gotten myself into?" Well, every time I came home to my beautiful wife and kids, I was reminded that I must continue making that sacrifice for my family. I was determined to stay true to myself and maintain my morals and values. Be cool and don't be no fool. Over the years, I've seen many inmates come and go. It's always rewarding to see a former gang member or criminal reform and rehabilitate himself by taking advantage of the many opportunities in educational and vocational classes. Displaying a strong desire to repent of their sins and study scriptures in religious services has helped many. Also, the recreational activities and peer support groups have taught many the importance of self-awareness, accountability, teamwork, and pulling together for a common goal.

A correctional officer wears many hats. I was a counselor, psychiatrist, teacher, preacher, medical assistant, first responder, EMT, cook, dishwasher, supervisor, coach, daddy, grand daddy, and much more. My whole life has been about reaching out to help others by volunteering and giving back to my community. I was raised to never look down on anyone and always be willing to lend a helping hand to those in need. So, in a funny way, this whole journey started with a food stamp. But in the end, it was my father's stamp of approval that propelled me towards my career in the Department of Corrections.

PROLOGUE

Dr. Frances Cres Welsing once said, "Racism is viewed as a global behavior power system with a constant and specific set of power relationships. Racism evolved with the singular goal of white supremacy or white power domination by the global white minority over the vast non-white global majority. The colored global collective has been forced into the position of relative powerlessness compared to the global white collective, establishing the power equation of white over non-white. Racism, whether consciously or unconsciously evolved as a survival necessity for the tiny global white minority, due to their genetic recessive status as albino variants (mutants) in a world of skin color genetically dominant black, brown, red, and yellow peoples. Indeed, had the global white minority not evolved this specific system of power relationships where whites control all of the behavior activity of non-whites in all areas of people activity (economics, education, entertainment, labor, law, politics, religion, sex and war) as a survival mechanism in the presence of the genetically dominant colored world majority, the mutant albino genetic recessive minority would find itself genetically annihilated. There would be no white people except for the new mutations to albinism produced by skin melanted or colored peoples. So to prevent white skin annihilation, a behavior power system of racism or white supreme domination evolved."[1]

---

[1] Dr. Frances Cres Welsing, "The Isis Papers" (Washington, D.C.: C.W. Publishing, 2004), preface.

PART I

PRISON LIFE

EXPOSING THE CRACKS

These poems are:

Politically incorrect
Grammatically incorrect

Unapologetically Black
Exposing unrepaired cracks

A little inspection
Inside prisons with no correction

Looking at humans full of rage
Locked inside a steel cage

State raised and produced
Buck broken and reduced

Medically induced
Heroin seduced

Shot into the veins
Numb to the pain

Penal system got rich
Profiting off the mentally sick

Living a nice suburban life
Thanks to the crack pipe

Gangs took over blocks
Slanging them crack rocks

Empowered young boys
Had real guns and no toys

Shot callers employ
To kill and destroy

It was all by design
To manipulate the young Black mind

Terrible tragedies hard to observe
By corrupt cops sworn to protect and serve

Laws protect them and there's no resistance
Pookie killed Ray Ray and got a life sentence

Pull the covers back and reveal the crooks
Wrote my thoughts down and put them in a book.

CHASING CHEESE

Sitting at my desk with a cup of coffee,
Sending out letters and making copies.

Tried to promote, scored high on the exam,
Had great interviews, but I wasn't in the plans.

Too black, too strong, they couldn't take it.
Passed on me because I couldn't fake it.

Getting tired of all the favoritism,
Walking into rooms full of racism.

Think I need a little vacation;
Take some time to assess the situation.

I'm not happy, feel like I'm getting robbed.
It's time for me to get another job.

I think I'll go in another direction;
Maybe I'll try the Department of Corrections.

I'm not sure if I should,
But I heard the money is good.

Priorities in place, take care of needs,
I have a young family to feed.

At the academy for sixteen weeks;
Man, it was hard to get some sleep.

Now I'm working in the joint;
Now it's time to prove my point

HIT THE GATE

Every day I wake up at four,
Dread every minute before I walk out the door.

I wash my face and brush my teeth,
Go to the kitchen and grab an apple to eat.

As I put on my uniform vest,
I hope today I can give my best.

Always in a hurry and running late;
Gotta show my I.D. at the main gate.

Lord, Lord, I come to pray,
Please bless me with a peaceful day.

Never know what's gonna happen at work;
I hope my partner is not a jerk.

Somedays are not so hard
When chillin' with the crew on the yard.

Somebody got to step up and do it;
I'll deliver mail to the housing unit.

Do what you say and say what you do,
Most inmates will respect you.

Sometimes they act a fool and clown;
Use common sense to calm things down.

Best thing to do is communicate,
Bust no heads, de-escalate.

That's all for now, I can't be late;
It's time for me to hit the gate.

WALK THE LINE

Hot on the yard when you walk the line,
Hope they don't hold me for overtime.
Sweatin' hard in the summertime;
A cold drink would be right on time.

Black inmates, separate Blood from Crips;
I can't believe they still doin' this shit.
Black on Black crimes need to quit.
Is Black Lives Matter really legit?

Most Hispanics in the same ride;
At L.A.C. it's the south side.
Still representing brown pride;
Still shanking homies when they lie.

They lay low, not out of sight,
Aryan peckerwoods make up the whites.
They are privileged and think they are right;
Protected now, they don't have to fight.

Not white, Hispanic or brotha,
It's a small group called "the others."
Samoans and Asians help one another,
Even Filipinos are getting tougher.

All of these groups have a lot of tricks;
They all play prison politics.
Going from zero to a hundred real quick,
Criminal mindset and still sick.

Every day on the hour
It's a constant struggle for power;
Lazy worker demanding a shower,
Actin' a fool yelling at the tower.

Need a doctor, head is aching,
Stand in line for medication.
E.O.P. yard, some are faking,
Rollin' blunts and meditating.

Searching cells for contraband,
Inmate had a needle in his hand;
Hiding weapons in his waistband,
Don't wanna get caught so he ran.

Cell phone hidden in a box of wafers,
Inmate weapon made from a sheet of paper.
Never know, might have to use it later,
Then go to the chapel to kneel in prayer.

Pics on the wall of tits and ass,
Rubbing meat as the time pass;
Look out the window through the thick glass,
All you see is dirt and dead grass.

Release dayroom, walk the tier,
Everyone out, have no fear.
Is that a cellphone I hear?
Tattooed face full of tears.

Often encouraged to do the right thing,
Some inmates can really sing.
Keep hope alive and pursue the dream;
Stay focused and build self-esteem.

Locked up for not obeying the law,
Didn't know some dudes can draw;
Chicano jail art was the best I saw;
No formal lessons, just self-taught.

Board up the door, cell extraction;
He ain't tough, he's pretending and acting.
Angry staff looking for action;
Put the shield on, he might be gassin'.

Assaults, stabbings, 2-on-1 fights,
In this environment, things are not right.
Yard lockdown because of a kite;
Back stabbing officers, they not tight.

When it gets real quiet,
Feels like we about to have a riot.
Weapons on the yard, tried to hide it,
Underhand toss, bombs are flying.

Yard alarm, everyone down;
Rack the mini, insert the rounds.
Gangsters fighting and running around,
Time for staff to put the yard down.

Damn I hate running to fights,
Blood and guts not a pretty sight.
Now I have to stay and write,
Looking in my bag for something to bite.

I hope the sergeant gives the okay,
Cuz I'm really done for the day,
And I'm not trying to stay.
Gotta go watch my son play.

TUFF LUV

Getting off the bus, wrist in chains,
Strollin' like a "G" 'bout to do this thang.

Ready for strip-out in R&R line;
Bend at the waist and cough three times.

Now it's time to hit the yard;
Did this before, this shit ain't hard.

Walk in the building to find my cell;
"What's up my nigg?" all the homies yell.

Go in my cell and do 100 burpies;
Got a sore on my lip, hope it ain't herpes.

Got a good workout, now I need a shower,
But I'm tired of calling the C/O tower.

I'm so hungry I could eat a cow;
I need to hurry up and get ready for chow.

Uugh! That was nasty and a hot mess;
They served us a tray of S.O.S.

I guess I'll make a noodle spread,
Watch some TV and go to bed.

I had a dream about my past;
So many things, my life is moving fast.

Momma in the kitchen, cooking rice;
Daddy outside shooting dice.

Eating baloney sammich on white bread;
Kool-Aid in a pickle jar, make it red.

We were poor, didn't have no toys;
Played ball in the streets with my boys.

Many memories growing up in the hood,
But I have to say it was not all good.

I really shouldn't be in this place,
But I was living that life in the rat race.

Now I sit in this rotten cell
Trying to live and not die in this hell.

I'm on the yard crew raking rocks;
A hundred degrees outside, damn it's hot!

Next I got a job in the kitchen,
Working hard for an extra piece of chicken.

Maybe I need to go to college,
Because I need more than prison knowledge.

I called my momma on my cell phone,
Told her I can't wait to get home.

She said be patient and do your time;
When you get out you will be fine.

Study and work hard every day;
Read your Bible, kneel, and pray.

Momma said she was tired of crying,
But when I get out the chicken will be frying.

That's what I need, a little tuff luv;
Now it's time to lean on the Man above.

BUSTED ON THE BLOCK

Purple drank sippin',
Black ass whippin',
No blood no crippin',
Sugar free pimpin'.

Always up to no good,
Pushing product in the hood;
In the batter's box I stood,
Always swinging big wood.

Pretty Toney loves the honeys;
Ain't a damn thing funny.
Today is Blue Monday;
Bitch betta have my money.

On the corner selling rock,
Got busted on the block;
Slanging dope to an undercover cop,
Cannabis in the medical shop.

Here we go again,
Doing time in the pen;
Can't be trusted, ain't got no friends,
Need a hustle to make ends.

Fights on the yard every day;
The game is real when you don't pay.
Read the Bible as I lay,
On my knees when I pray.

Throwin' punches, legs kickin',
Shank in hand, ready for stickin'.
Sliced him up like a piece of chicken;
Bitch made nigga, now he trickin'.

Now I'm sittin' in the hole;
No blanket or sheets, damn it's cold.
Raggedy mattress in a roll;
Man, this shit is getting old.

LOCKDOWN

They locked us down on a bogus kite;
Now bring us up, this shit ain't right.

Tired of taking bird baths in the sink;
I need to get out, cuz this cell stinks.

Gotta stand up and get off this bed,
Walk around a bit and stretch my legs.

Don't wanna eat no more stale bread;
Second draw canteen, I need to get fed.

I don't know how many books I read;
Can't get enough knowledge in my head.

TV went out, ain't got no power;
I need a sergeant ... help me out, Tower.

Ain't got no apples to make my drank;
Gotta keep busy working on this shank.

Thinking 'bout my girl, I'll write a love letter;
Looking at her picture makes me feel better.

Maybe I need to stop all of this wishing;
Make me a good string and go tier fishing.

Play some dominos or break out the cards,
Gotta do something cuz we ain't going to yard.

What I really need is something to smoke,
Cuz this lockdown is a fugging joke.

SLIDE A NEEGA A BURRITO

One by one they came walking back,
Kicking rocks while walking the track.

What's going on? What did they serve?
It was some bullshit, and it's getting on my nerve.

I ain't got no food; I need to go to the sto.
Hey man, "Slide a neega a burrito."

I'm so broke ain't got no bread;
Tired of eating soups and noodle spreads.

I really didn't want to go;
Can you "Slide a neega a burrito"?

Week after week it's the same old shit:
Biscuits for breakfast, hard as bricks.

Apples and peanut butter on pancakes,
Wish it was syrup and butter on the plate.

Fell off my tray and hit the flo;
I just kicked my green Jell-O.

Dumped the tray and walked out the dough;
Yo, "Slide a neega a burrito."

Every Sunday we get cell fed:
Potatoes, sausage, cereal, and eggs.

Half warm and sometimes cold,
Damn this menu is getting old.

Sometimes the chow line is really long,
Especially when they serve chicken on the bone.

Most of the time it's the same old thing:
Peas, carrots, rice, and beans

But on this day they had cabbage and meatballs;
Trash that bullshit in the chow hall.

Now, there's one thing I got to know:
Can you "Slide a neega a burrito"?

PUTTIN' THE SMACK DOWN

On the streets he took no flack;
Pimp hand strong, bitch he smacked.
He gettin' money and stackin' racks;
The hood goin' crazy from smokin' crack.

Pistol clip grippin',
Ghost ride whippin',
Malt liquor sippin',
Grand hustle pimpin'.

Now he locked up, don't ask why;
Speakin' the truth, tellin' no lies.
Wishin' he had a bean pie;
Still got wings, ready to fly.

Still poppin' his collar,
Not makin' a dollar.
Drops knowledge like a scholar,
Hittin' hard like a brawler.

The only man on planet Mars,
Followin' the crescent moon and star.
Vision is deep, can see very far;
He is at peace, but ready for war.

Every day he reads the Quran,
Listens to the minister Farrakhan.
Doin' his time teachin' everyone,
Strong belief a new day will come.

IS REAL

Is he real?
Filing daily inmate appeals?

Blind with the stick, using his feel;
Seeing through the bullshit, he knows the deal.

Ain't got no money but has all of the bills;
Fighting for his rights with plenty of zeal.

No medication, takes no pill;
Older guy, but never gets ill.

Tried to take him out like Emmett Till,
Boxing in his cell ready to kill.

Mind is sharp, Black man still;
Gonna take a lot to break his will.

Talk to Jack and his partner Jill;
They will tell you he is real.

E-O MUTHAFUGGIN P

Hey, C/O, I talked to the laundry lady;
She said we can exchange today.
Can I go? Is it okay?
I didn't hear you. What did you say?

Stand by? What does that mean?
Wait? Damn, I need some purple lean.
Can't drink, I'm s'pose to stay clean;
Fugg it, I ain't part of the team.

Damn C/O, you lazy;
I'm 'bout to go crazy.
It's getting kinda hazy;
Can't let this shit faze me.

I'm a killa
From the Black Gorilla;
Bananas I peela,
Thrilla in Manilla

I'm E-O Muthafuggin P;
You don't wanna see me.
Open my door, set me free;
I gotta change my dirty laundry.

I'm a muthafuggin S.N.Y.
Till I muthafuggin die.
I eat sweet potato pie;
I believe I can fly.

What? You aint gonna let me out?
What is this all about?
Why I gotta scream and shout?
I'm gonna bust a cap and leave no doubt.

I'm an E-O Muthafuggin P gangsta!
I ain't no pranksta.
No muthafuggin wanksta;
Please open my door, I thank ya

CAN I GET A CRACK

Hey, C/O, can I get a crack?
I'll be fast and I'll close it right back.

Hey, C/O, can I get a crack?
My boy making burritos; they in a big sack.

Hey, C/O, can I get a crack?
It's right by the door in a stack.

Hey, C/O, can I get a crack?
This is the last time, gimme some slack.

Hey, C/O, can I get a crack?
Can't slide it under the door, it's in a pack.

Hey, C/O, can I get a crack?
Give a brotha a break—look, I'm Black.

Hey, C/O, can I get a crack?
I'm messin' up, but I'll get on track.

Hey, C/O, can I get a crack?
You didn't open the door; man, that's wack.

I'M A PORTER

Pop my door cuz I'm a no limit soulja;
Workin' hard as a second watch porter.

Movin' down the tier in my running shoes;
Sweatin' hard in my California State blues.

I'm the lead man, that's what you need to know;
Pushin' brooms, swingin' mops, and cleanin' the floor.

I pass out all of the toilet paper and soap;
I bless the building, but I'm no pope.

I'm a boss, but I'm no Ricky Ross.
Pop my collar, cuz everday I'm tryna floss.

In my cell I got a hot pot cookin' rice,
On the tier playin' the dozens and rollin' dice.

Some think I'm only into distribution,
Passin' out fish kits to newbies in the institution.

Every day I'm hustlin' up and down the tier;
I've been doin' this shit for twenty-five years.

Pop the door so I can clean the shower;
I always do them, same time this hour.

Proud of my work, my mop stroke is long;
Take a rest as I sit on my throne.

Lean back with my white robe on;
Nice and clean, the dayroom is my home.

I stay Black and I stay strong.
I'm a country pimp; I ain't did nothin' wrong.

I'm done now, I'm gonna leave you alone;
Good day, sir, take care, I'm gone.

HITTIN' THE CELL

Don't cry like a bitch
When yo cell get hit.

They always get mad when you go in their cell;
Well, stop collecting all of those apples in the pail.

Don't wanna go in the muthafugga because it stank,
But I know you been in there making shanks.

I do my job; I don't stutter.
Why you hiding your phone in peanut butter?

Expensive phone yo momma bought,
It's not my fault you got caught.

Some officers get real mad
When you have water bags.

I don't like seeing the pants sag,
Still tryna bang with a rag.

Incense burning, smell like skunk,
But I can still smell the blunt.

Found another bag with pruno chunks,
Getting it ready to pass to the drunks.

Everybody running around on speed,
And the building always smells like weed.

Don't do drugs is the warning to heed,
No reefer, no shoebox, no seeds.

Don't cover your window with cardboard;
You can't hide your canteen store.

What's all this shit on the floor?
Clotheslines everywhere, rags tore.

Turn off your hot pot, water vapors.
Why do you have twenty toilet papers?

It ain't that bad, don't act like you dying;
It's a new day, that's no denying.

Inmates need to stop all of that crying;
It's lunchtime, I smell baloney frying.

BEGGIN' A BITCH

What's up, girl, how you doing today?
When are you gonna come out and play?
You owe me a visit; I know you can't stay.
I'm stuck in this cage with my cellie all day.

One day I will get out;
I'm gonna scream and shout,
Show you what I'm all about,
Give it all to you and leave no doubt.

Can't wait to open your thighs,
Fugg you hard, deep inside,
Spank dat ass and hear your cries,
Hold you close, feel my size.

Baby don't give that pussy away;
Please save it for me, okay?
Cuz i'm gonna beat it up every day;
You can't leave me, no way.

When I get out, we gonna do the damn thing;
Take you downtown and get you a ring.
You are my queen, and I am your king,
Most beautiful girl I've ever seen.

But there's one thing I got to tell you, honey:
You're so cute, my little bunny.
Coming from me, this might sound funny,
But can you please send me some money?

I really feel like a dummy;
Calling you like this is kinda bummy.
Lost it all playing gin rummy;
Ain't got no bread, just crummies.

Had a stroke of bad luck,
Now I feel like I'm stuck.
I really need a few bucks;
Neega's on my back, I'm tryna duck.

I remember you told me you got a lot of bills;
Hard out there, I know how you feel.
But I gotta keep it real;
Please send the cheese, if you will.

Can you hurry up? I can't wait.
Things are getting ugly; I can feel the hate.
Gotta pay my dues, I'm already late;
When I pay you back, we going on a big date.

C'mon, put the money on my books;
When I get out, I'll wash dishes and cook,
Let you know how good you look.
I'll be good; I won't be a crook.

Hell naw, I don't wanna hear that shit.
What do you mean you can't do it?
I'm pissed! I'm about to throw a fit;
I thought you was my bottom bitch.

You supposed to hold me down;
You making me look like a clown.
I'm not happy, you making me frown;
I'm tryna swim, but you gonna let me drown.

I take it all back, you ain't my boo;
Stupid bitch, you don't know what to do.
I remember the time you fugged my crew;
As a matter of fact, I'm done with you.

The Reply:

Are you finished with your little spiel?
Really? That's how you feel?
You sound like a pig when you squeal;
Neega, I told you I got a lot of bills.

You a selfish muthafugga;
Hope you get yo ass kicked, sucka.
No mo ass kissin', lips don't pucka;
With me, you ran out of lucka.

All of these years you played me like a fool;
My momma told me to go back to school.
She said you used me like a tool;
It's my fault, I didn't follow the rules.

I tried to wait around for you,
But yo daddy called and I fugged him too.
Sugar daddy buys me new shoes;
He does everything you are supposed to do.

So warm up them soups on your hot plate;
Thinking about you while I eat shrimp and steak.
Don't get mad, don't playa hate,
Cuz today is a brand-new day.

So get off your knees crying;
Stop acting like you're dying.
I'm tired of your bitchin' and lying,
Cuz your shit I ain't buying.

GETTIN' IT IN

There was a girl named Beth;
She used to bring in meth.
She had crooked teeth and bad breath;
They put her to the test.

She had no class,
but she hid the stash.
Put the dope in her ass,
Pussy smell like sea bass.

Another one named Cindy
Hid the dope under her tiddy.
She was kinda pretty,
but her attitude was shitty.

She was a white girl;
She was down with the swirl.
She liked diamonds and pearls;
He rocked her world.

They came in every week;
They never missed a beat.
They played with the meat;
They could take the heat.

Next week called a friend;
Her name was Gwen.
She had a twin;
They both came in.

Checked in at the gate;
Had a long wait.
But their spirit didn't break;
They really looked great.

She brought him some weed,
Hid it under her weave.
Still hard to believe
Just met her last week.

Called his bottom bitch;
She act like she rich.
Gave him a tongue kiss,
Then he swallowed "it."

Dirty hands dusted,
She's the one he trusted.
Big ass he lusted;
Almost got busted.

Visiting over, gotta go;
She driving back to Fresno.
Thanked her for bringing in the dough;
Next week called another hoe.

She's a bad Latina;
Her name is Gina.
Don't call her a beana;
Comes from Pasadena.

Stanky finga creama;
Put her hand on the weena.
She's a pipe cleana;
Put her on the teama.

Pretty eyes gleama;
Don't sleep on a dreama.
She wanted to bringa;
iPhone ringa.

What the fugg?
Grandmomma in cuffs
For bringing in stuff.
C/O talking to her tuff.

She had "it" under her wig;
This was her Sunday service gig.
The payoff was big;
She had more in her diaper hid.

Don't ask her why;
She can't remember her lie.
She gettin' milked dry;
Should be at home baking a pie.

Lil' old sweet lady
Would do anything for her baby.
Shot-gun Sally is shady;
She ain't stupid, but this shit is crazy.

Back on the yard
Inmates tryna act hard.
Old warriors with a lot of scars
Doing dips and pull ups on bars.

The nurse gave him some lube;
It was in a little tube.
That's what he used
To hoop the balloons.

He wiped the dirt off his shoes,
Hung up his prison blues,
Listened to the same old news
And paid his dues.

Then he asked the Tower
If he can get a shower.
Didn't wanna smell sour
Cuz chow begins in an hour.

PASSIN' OUT CONDOMS

Passin' out condoms,
But I can't have no drank.
I can't make a shank;
I can't smell like stank.

Passin' out condoms,
But a girl you can't fugg.
Shim got the weenie tucked;
Say hello to deez nutz.

Passin' out condoms,
Sugar level always high.
Red Kool-Aid hair dye,
Wearing a ponytail twisted to the side

Passin' out condoms,
No sucky, no tits.
Just dicks and no chicks;
Just sticks and no slits.

Passin' out condoms,
Hard to believe
Adam still tryna fugg Steve.
No pussy, no Eve.

Passin' out condoms,
Porters hustlin', jailhouse rich.
Tryna make a dolla out of fifteen cents,
Neck tattooed, "fugg a bitch."

Passin' out condoms
Wit no bitch is whack.
Might as well sell needles in a pack
To junkies still trickin' for smack.

Passin out condoms
But can't go on a date.
Use a rubber, hope it don't break;
No glove, no love, said the state.

GREEN FISH

She was ready for the beat,
Boots polished on her feet,
Uniform nice and neat.

She's an Academy grad;
She gave it all she had.
Now she wears a shiny badge.

She had a smile on her face,
Displayed style and grace,
Getting ready for the rat race.

She's a pretty young thang,
Mouths open, tongues hang,
Everybody wanna bang.

She got weekends off, admin spot,
Running errands for Sergeant a lot,
Hoping that she don't get got.

But she don't know
They'll cook her nice and slow
Till she's ready to go.

Latina, white, or sista,
Tom cats can't resist her;
She's a fish fry flipper.

But she's a green fish,
The last on the list,
Got held over and now she's pissed.

Now she's starting to get around,
Running with a pack of horny hounds,
Behind her back they clown.

Smiles turn to frowns,
Head and shoulders down,
Cuz she's getting passed around.

Frustrated and bitter,
She's a one hitter quitter.
Don't swallow, just a spitter.

Pinned down on her back,
Gettin' dick slapped
While jugglin' nut sacks.

Hard core, no affection,
Feminine side neglecting,
Always mad as protection.

She worked her way to the top
Getting used as a thot,
Sitting in the captain's spot.

Now she's a boss;
Promotion came with a cost.
Self-respect is lost.

BUMP AND MUMP

There was a cop by the name of Bump,
Training his rookie partner how to hump.

Always looking for cuffed inmates to dump,
Braggin' to co-workers, his chest is pumped.

Igniting shit to make a neega jump,
Running to the sergeant like Forrest Gump.

Buck dancing for the man, faking the krump,
Padding stats in his report to make it look plump.

No alarms today, his shoulders are slump;
Tearing up cells, acting like a grump.

Couldn't find nothing, now he stumped,
Bitching and complaining to his partner, Mump.

Mump acting like he wanna give out some lumps;
He ain't bout that action cuz he's a chump.

Bump's an Uncle Tom kissin' rump;
His dumb ass voted for Tump.

He's a phony, he don't wanna thump;
He down low, humping Mump.

BLACKBALLED

The real story has rarely been told
About the Black officer on the slave patrol.

Unscrew your black balls,
Hang 'em up on the green wall.

Lose all of your Black pride
If you wanna get on the ride

Forget what you learned at the Academy;
That's not what we do here actually.

Welcome to a life of grief and agony.
Watch your back; don't become a casualty.

There's no treats, just tricks;
Learn what makes the monster tick.

You need to become a prick and join a clique;
Promotion comes quick with daily ass licks.

You see many birds and different feathers;
Dirty cops fly together.

Blurred vision distorts what you see,
Desensitize yourself from empathy.

But a blind man can see the rejection
Of inmates with dark complexion.

Unorganized with no direction,
Unplugged with no connection.

No juice, no protection,
Infiltrated with infection.

On this modern-day slave ship,
Crakkkas give you the whip.

They expect you to follow the script,
Beat down all Bloods and Crips.

Watch the Black Gorillas on the plantation,
Give favors to members of the Aryan nation.

Compromise with the Mexicans;
Reprimand the Africans.

Always push a hard line
On your own kind.

If you show any compassion,
You will get a harsh reaction.

Labeled "hug a thug,"
Suspected of smuggling drugs.

If you give 'em extra covers,
They'll call you an inmate lover.

Don't give 'em nothing, let 'em suffer,
Hung out to dry if you help a brotha.

They want a Boondoc Uncle Ruckas
Selling out to these evil suckas.

"Sucka neega," said Tribe,
Like Eddie and Martin doing Life.

Gun line ready, boss.
Nail them neegas to the cross.

After work, some partners go to the gym,
One brotha in the group tryna fit in.

Walking, talking, and acting like them,
A raisin in a bowl of oatmeal, with a cheesy grin.

But when there's a leak in the engine,
Low morality builds with hostility and tension.

Black officer now scared to speak up;
He's told to shut the fugg up.

All of a sudden, they need support;
Work as a team to write bogus reports.

It was all a foolish game
That blew up in flames.

He pretended to be tuff
Until investigators slapped on them cuffs.

Stickin' with the lie sealed his fate,
Shamefully getting walked out the gate.

He wasn't prepared to take the fall;
Played himself when he gave up his balls.

No mo friends, nobody to call;
Punk ass neega got blackballed.

TOY SOLDIERS

Elbow deep in ass, lifting balls,
Pushing the inmate face-first against the wall.
Aggressive pat down, almost made him fall;
Not that serious, don't start a brawl.

That's the get down in building one,
Where wheelchairs roll and porters run,
Lookouts waiting for the punks to come,
Mac rep and porter business is done.

It's a constant reminder that they are in jail,
Afraid of C/O's hittin' their cell.
Contraband, weapons, snitches tell,
Locked in a maze, kept under a spell.

Toy soldiers really ain't tuff;
It's all a big ass bluff.
They don't want it to get real ruff
While walking the tier strutting their stuff.

Donut and cake bringing
Sergeant nut swinging
On his leg clinging
Tweety bird singing

Info leaking
Pruno sweeping
Side door sneaking
C/O's creeping

Soft ass prison guards
Running real hard
Cuz they heard an alarm,
Bullshit fight on the yard.

A couple of cops sprayed,
Some threw grenades.
Nobody threw a fade;
Didn't wanna get laid.

FAKE ASS SARJENT

It's the calm before the storm.
All of the yard kops began to swarm
To the housing unit alarm.
1-on-1 fight, no harm.

But the top kop on the yard
Is trying real hard
To ride in the Sarjent's car.
He thinks he's a star

Always talking 'bout kicking butt,
Tryna prove he got big nuts,
Acting like he gives no fucks,
But when shit happens, he has bubble guts.

He really wants to be a boss,
Always on the radio tryna floss.
All of his self-pride is lost;
Doesn't know it comes with a cost.

Hanging out with the Sar-jent
At the river pitching tents.
Roasting wieners at the fire pit,
Drinking beer from the money he spent.

He starting to believe his own hype,
Walking the yard with invisible stripes.
At the computer ready to type,
Bending for the LT taking the pipe.

But it all ended so sad
Because he gave it all he had.
Now he comes to work mad,
Fake ass Sarjent with no badge.

POISON COOLAIDE

Smile in their face, stab 'em in the back;
Hit 'em with the Whopper, not a Big Mac.
A wolf in sheep's clothing, don't believe the act.

Bullshit in the skillet, pan fry,
Spoon-fed knee grows digesting the lie,
Getting pumped up to believe they can fly.

Like Jimm Jones led them astray,
Serving deadly cups of Poison Coolaide,
Get in line for the baloney buffay.

One-stop shop at cell 119,
At his door you can get anything,
Canteen ice cream for the Dairy Queens

Acting like the great white hope,
Passing out the toilet paper and soap,
Without him they can't cope.

He kissin' ass every day
To get an extra food tray.
Most C/O's let him have his way.

On the tier running the block,
Fixing radios, watches, and clocks,
Thinks he's untouchable, can't be stopped.

Hooking up televisions and broken fans,
For C/O's, he collects the cans.
He really thinks he's the man.

But he's just another porter,
Acts like he's above taking orders
From a real soul brotha.

While dumping the trash and sweeping the floor,
He is told to go close his door,
But he's on a mission and totally ignores.

Hey, C/O, I need a crack;
Got these burritos in a sack.
Did you say no? Is it because I'm not black?

Order my tray, make that call,
Cuz I don't eat in the chow hall.
I'm entitled and above all.

The happy helper is his bait,
Looking for victims to manipulate.
You can never trust a friendly snake.

Not a real witness, just another fake
Pretending to follow Watchtower and Awake,
Bows his head to pray for another victim to slay.

SNITCHIN 'N' BITCHIN

The rhymes I be spittin'
Is about punks on the yard snitchin'.
A bunch of grown men bitchin'
On the hoe stroll switchin'.

Hidin' out like a chicken,
Owing money caught slippin,
Nervous as fugg, always twichin',
Runnin' to the captain steady snitchin'.

Jailhouse vags, now they trickin',
Tossin' salad, asshole lickin',
Raggedy hoe, ridin' dickin',
Lip gloss on, ass be kissin'.

Now he sick, barely kickin',
HIV/Hep-C stricken,
Dirty needles stickin',
Time bomb tickin'.

No kites, but still tippin',
Dirty ass rats straight flippin',
Watered down Bloods, broken ass Crippin',
Weak ass neegas slippin' and trippin'.

Programs all day, still be bitchin',
Got fugged up on the yard, now he limpin',
In the cage with demons and wiccan,
Shank in hand, throats be slittin'.

This is where all the woods be kickin',
Weapons sharp, Hispanics be stickin',
Blacks divided ain't no clickin',
It's a yard full of snitchin' 'n' bitchin'.

CHILLIN' ON THE HONOR YARD

The fight is over, no more war,
No sticking, no stabbing, just old scars.
It's so easy, it ain't that hard,
When you chillin' on the honor yard.

A level three
Is the place to be;
It's hard to believe
They acting friendly.

Former Ad-Seg mask spitters
Always walked around mad and bitter,
Angry one hitter quitters
Now peaceful crochet knitters.

Went to the hole again and again;
Did hard time in the pen.
Made weapons to batter men;
Now making scarfs for battered women.

Wards of the State, acted a fool,
Programming now and following the rules.
No more sharp weapon tools;
Sharpening their minds, going to school.

Getting up off the knees,
Some shims, no shes;
Drinking black coffee,
Acting like they free.

The sky is clear, no fog;
Inmates going for a morning jog.
Walking around the track with a dog,
A lot of baloney, but no hog.

Most of them got life
With no stress or strife,
No smoke from the pipe,
Ain't flying no kites.

Dogs don't bite,
No reports to write,
Just smack, no hype,
They got yard at night.

Tennis shoe pimps tryna flex,
Long t-shirts they dress.
In dayroom the game is chess,
But dominos slam the best.

Behind the wall, P.I.A.
Sweeping the dirt, ballgame today.
Drums in the band, ready to play;
Porters hustlin' big food tray.

Visits with the fam,
Got a girl named Pam,
Big ass full of ham,
Small waist, gahh damn!

They get a lot of program;
The yard is never slammed.
Jelly sammich, no jam,
Not Denny's but a grand slam

Everything seems to be going well,
Pizza and chicken food sale.
They eating good locked up in jail;
Inmates got a lot of stories to tell.

Can you open the door please?
New laws make them believe
That they are going to leave.
They got everything but the keys.

PART II

STRUGGLE 'N' STRIFE

THE BLACK CRACK ATTACK

Every Saturday he washed that Cadillac;
Beautiful ride, black on black.
Got laid off, now it's sittin' on flats;
Down and depressed, he started smoking crack.

His kids out all night, hanging out in the back;
His home was nice, now it looks like a shack.
Always broke, can't afford a Big Mac;
Bill collectors calling, catching a lot of flack.

Down the street was Ms. Judy;
She had a big ol' juicy booty.
Her husband was tooty fruity;
Tending the garden was her duty.

Her man left her for a dude name Larry;
Now she on the pipe, fugg that fairy.
She was pretty, now she looks scary;
Ten-dollar blow jobs, she's a strawberry.

They boil the shit till it's hot,
Stir the jar in a big ass pot.
Then they sell it on the block;
Now the hustlers got them rocks.

An addictive cheap high,
Some believed they could fly.
Smoke enough till you die;
In the casket you lie.

Lookouts on the block, pockets fatter;
Here comes the police, everybody scatter.
Hide the dope in the cookie batter;
All about the money, nothing else matters.

It's a cold game that turns even colder,
Always looking over your shoulder.
This life makes you bad and bolder,
But in the blink of an eye, it could be over.

Bad in them streets,
Everybody carrying heat.
Gotta be quick on your feet;
Don't know who you might meet.

Pimps and hustlers making big money
In the club with all of the fly honeys.
Got a house on the hill, don't live in the slummys;
Puttin' steak, shrimp, and lobster in his tummy.

All of the homies in the crew getting paid;
Fuggin bitches every day getting laid.
Guns loaded, knives sharp on the blade,
Music bumpin', fat rims on the escalade.

While hangin' on the block,
Slim and his boy got popped
By an undercover cop.
Pulled out his gun and made 'em drop.

Ain't no snitchin', nobody tell;
Looks like they 'bout to go to jail.
The party's over, everybody going to hell;
Gave his momma money, but she can't post bail.

Now why did he start selling drugs?
Grew up poor, no lights to plug.
Rat and roaches, house full of bugs,
Moms and Pops gave out no hugs.

He acts like he don't care;
Deadbeat left and disappeared.
Momma on the couch, braiding hair,
Tryna make ends on welfare.

So he started making money fast,
No job, no check, just straight cash.
Buying clothes, jewelry, and smoking grass;
Little did he know this shit wouldn't last.

BATTER RAM

Give the children medication,
Bad schools, poor education,
Brainwashed manipulation,
HIV hits the nation.

Kids growin' up with no dad;
Momma is all they had.
Getting in trouble, acting bad,
Emotionally disturbed, always mad.

Flood the hood with dope;
Give them neegas no hope.
No jobs, they can't cope;
Kick 'em down, foot on the throat.

Drankin' 40 ounce,
Dippin' to more bounce,
Fat burger pounce,
Rival hood trounce.

Parliament, flashlight,
Mary Jane, pop life,
Joints, bongs, crack pipes,
Late at night, ready to fight.

Big crews gangbanging;
Big ballers dope slanging.
Big gold chains hanging;
Big cell phones ranging.

Where did the guns come from?
Everybody and they momma had one.
The gubbament was mum;
The Prez was Ronald Ray-gun.

A midnight mission was the plan;
Bust down the door with the Batter Ram.
Helmets, guns, big boom bam;
Five-o came, everybody ran.

The El Ay Pee Dee
Killing brothas in the street;
Shot him in the back when he tried to flee;
Crooked cops got off free.

Black man hate
Chief Darrel Gate.
High crime rate,
33 pens in the State.

A lot of drug bust,
From smoking angel dust;
Mental institutions shut,
Fill the prisons up.

Jheri curl perm
Looking like Big Worm;
Strung out on the sherm,
With a long prison term.

Part of the master plan
Is to lock up the Black man.
Beat him down, cut off his hands;
Kill our sistas like Sandra Bland.

Some are dead, some are in prison;
Got caught up, now they in the system.
Sitting in the cell on the tier fishing;
Hoping to get out, praying and wishing.

Modern day plantation,
Mass incarceration,
Has fed the nation.
Capitalism is the explanation.

So everybody got fat
From slanging that crack;
Now the bullseye is on the back
On all the Blacks doing smack

SON DOWN

Every day the news gets sadder;
Crime pays, rich man fatter.
Bullets fly, people scatter.
Is it true, Black lives madder?

Hands up, don't shoot;
Getting stomped by the boot.
Flags in the air, don't salute;
Trash in the street, don't pollute.

Put in the clip,
Aiming to hit.
Let her rip,
Backbone split.

As the hot sun goes down
Another brotha is gunned down;
Lying in the street, middle of town,
All of the people gathered around.

Momma buried another son;
Tears flowed as the choir song.
Now she worried about her youngest one;
If she loses him, she's left with none.

SET TRIPPIN'

Big time tippin',
Parking lot pimpin',
Fish and shrimpin',
Ice cream drippin'.

In the club primpin',
Hoe's be strippin',
On the pole flippin',
Ass thong skimpin'.

Toe nail clippin',
Punks be wimpin',
Bitch fight nippin',
Swap meet jippin'.

Midnight dippin',
Candy paint whippin',
Don't get caught slippin',
Hand gun grippin'.

Manchester zippin',
Gin and juice sippin',
Eight Tray crippin',
He set trippin'.

CHICKEN HENNESSEE WEED

Chicken:
Roasted, baked, smothered or fried,
Mac and cheese with greens on the side.
Smackin' lips with each bite;
Mama made it, I know it's all right

Some say it's fanga lickin'
Is CFK straight trickin'?
Did they run out of chicken?
Is the kernal trippin'?

Most people really like
The crispy crunch of Pop-ize.
Sweet tea, beans, and rice;
Mild, hot, plenty of spice.

No bones to toss,
Tender bird, no need to floss.
Chicken legs and hot sauce,
Big Momma's chicken still the boss.

Yard-walker fattened for the kill,
No recipe needed, prepared with skill.
Eat everything on the chicken but the bill,
And that's chicken still.

Hennessee:
Take it to the back
When you drankin' that yak.
Don't know how to act
With a bottle in yo sack.

Mu fuggas trip
When they keep takin' sips;
Even Grandma got some nip
Hidden under her slip.

The numba 1 brand is Hennessee,
From the west coast to Tennessee.
Pastor drankin' at the jubilee
Tent revival ministry.

Glasses clinkin',
Breath be stinkin',
Red eyes blinkin',
Good times drinkin'.

Feelin' kinda tipsy,
The favorite drank of many.
The liquor store has plenty;
Gotta have that Henny.

Weed:
Rollin zig zags
With friends smokin' grass.
Puff, puff, pass,
Gettin' high fast.

Kush man hunt,
Hit it, don't bunt.
Playas don't stunt
When you smokin' a fat blunt.

Big money bizness
From the cannabis;
They legalized it,
White man get rich.

Don't get stopped,
Cuz brothas get caught
By undercover cops
For having a lot of pot.

Some brothas act as if it's a need;
Can't go a day without blazing the weed.
Highly addicted to the marijuana leaf;
Altered perception from THC.

NEEGARITIS

Eating plates of bullshit every day,
Force-fed lies, acting like it's okay,
Digesting bullets of govament gun play,
Black bloated bodies of death and decay.

White devil in the church, bullets spray;
Dead bodies on the ground, worshipers lay;
Next Sunday service, church members pray;
Forgive and forget, everybody's okay.

You neegas get on that field and do your best;
Better not be no flag protest.
You getting' paid to pass the test;
Do it again I'll cut your ass next.

Black players scared to fight it,
Froze with fear and frightened.
Big teeth, but afraid to bite it;
Lazy ass neegas got Neegaritis.

Bellies are full, mouths shut,
Eyes wide open, don't give a fugg.
Million dollar slaves don't have much;
Racist owners whipping their butt.

Riding in a Benz
With no money to spend;
Black tilted brim,
Black with silver trim.

Riding in a Benz,
Taking the whip for a spin.
Rocking twenty-four-inch rims,
Fake ballers just pretend.

Neegas standing in line for hours to vote;
Casting their ballot for the next white hope.
Rising tides has never lifted a black boat;
Demoncrats and Republiklans are a joke.

Making false promises to get in the Whyte Howse;
Can't believe a damn thing coming from their mouth.
The trap is set, a piece of cheese for the mouse;
Deceiving poor neegas in the deep south.

Tump was in office, sitting on the planet,
A wealthy apprentice wearing a new jacket.
Right wing militia group magnet;
If you Black, get back, damn it.

Neegas in the street high fiving,
Sipping yak and electric sliding.
No Vaseline, raw prick riding,
With Gem Krow Jo Bye-den.

Hoodrat talking out of the side of her neck,
Babysitting, braiding hair, and a welfare check.
Dishes piled high, house is a mess,
Shaking her ass, twerking the best.

Always paying her rent late,
Even though she living on section 8.
Weave down her back, long nails fake,
Baby daddy in the pen, living upstate.

No pots on the stove, can't cook;
Watching TV all day, won't read a book.
No pimps, no stroll, but know how to hook;
Small waist, fat ass, got neegas shook.

Cherry slurpy slurping,
Chicken biscuit burping,
Broke pimp flirting,
No money, pockets hurting.

Skinny jeans wearing, off the ass hanging,
Don't work still slanging.
Don't own the block, but still claiming;
Killing their brothas and still banging.

Crabs in a barrel, neegas hate;
Sitting on their ass, always late.
Scratching lotto tickets for a big break;
A Black mind is a terrible thing to waste.

NO MO ASS KISSIN'

Look in the mirror, stop lying;
You ain't no monkey, stop signifying.
Get off your knees, begging and crying.
Why you still shucking and jiving?

Just gotta make that white man happy;
Brown nosing yo massa, calling him Pappy.
Yo hair ain't straight, yo shit is nappy;
Buck dancing all the time, you look sappy.

Pearly white teeth grinning,
Yassa boss pretending,
Mulatto light skinning,
You think you winning.

Good golly wolly,
A puppet stringed dolly,
Always acting jolly,
Tap dancing for Mista Cholly.

On his leg like a leech,
Hate your color, now you bleach.
Dark cookie Oreo speech,
Joining the country club is a reach.

All aboard, the train is coming soon;
You neegas ain't going to the moon.
Winter in America don't come in June;
Stop acting like a muthafugging coon.

Eyes wide open, but still sleep;
Lost in a cave real deep.
Dignity and pride can't keep;
Stand in line, fugged like sheep.

Some things are still the same;
Selling your soul for fame,
It's a low-down dirty shame.
Sugar in the tank, plenty of flame.

Sipping on patrone
As you guard the throne;
And don't see nothing wrong.
Acting like you at home

On that old road to nowhere
But pushing real hard to get there,
Hoping that he really cares,
Just anotha house neega he can spare.

So stop doing cartwheels;
Let's keep it real.
Educate yourself, know the deal;
Whitey don't care how you feel.

Stars in the sky, don't be wishin';
Have self-pride, that's what's missin'.
Shhh!!! Be quiet and listen;
Stop all of that ass kissin'!!!

THE MARCH OF CRIMES

Neighborhood hustler sellin' CDs
Bumrushed to the ground by two police.
Shot him dead in the chest, now he bleeds,
Videotaped for the world to see.

Busted tail light was all it took
For racist police to act like crooks.
License, registration, he tried to look;
Shot and killed, she put it on Vasebook.

Pop, pop, pop, pop!
One by one they dropped.
1-8-7 on the undercover cop.
Five dead now, they want the violence to stop

Hands up, don't shoot, they sang;
Marches across the country began.
Non-violent protest was the plan;
Pull the trigger, kill again.

All of that marching, haven't moved one step;
Police still killing Blacks with led.
Undertaker still burying the dead;
Mommas crying over innocent bloodshed.

One way to get the murders to stop,
People get together and start a boycott.
Power to the people is all we got;
Gotta strike now while the iron is hot.

No work, no gas, that's a start;
No fast-food drive thrus, no Wollmart.
Rallying the people is the hard part;
Let's get organized and ignite the spark.

No football games in the coming weeks;
It can't start without the Black athletes.
Boycott on the field with no cleats;
Million dollar slaves not for sale on TV.

No wig, no weave, no nail shop;
No beer, no liquor, no weed spots.
Neckbones and beans straight from the pot;
Try it for a few days, you saving a lot.

All about stopping the cash flow;
Hurt their pockets, don't spend your dough.
Boycotting is the way to go,
Cuz we ain't taking it no mo.

HEAR THE CRIES

Pulling the trigger was all it took;
Cold blooded murder, the nation was shook.
Terrible tragedy, it was a hard look

Drove by with a gun in hand;
Aimed the pistol and shot the old man.
He was just picking up cans.

Gahhh damn!!!
He got back in the car and scrammed,
A wanted killer was on the lam.

Armed and dangerous, he might shoot;
Running for days, hungry for food.
Decided on a fast-food drive thru.

Couldn't wait, fries wasn't hot;
The workers hurried and called the cops.
Died from self-inflicted gun shot.

We are living in a world of hate,
With an evil criminal mind state.
Emotionally fragile, ready to break.

Psyche meds and mental health,
Financial troubles far from wealth,
Broken down, can't care for self.

No love, no family
No heart, no sympathy
No culture, no identity

Living with no hope,
Sitting around smoking dope,
Can't pay bills, can't cope.

Terrorized and kidnapped from a land forgotten;
Ancestors on plantations picking cotton,
Tried to fight back, but the whip was poppin'.

Life is hell, plenty of drama;
Crakkkas raping yo wife and momma,
Hanging neegas in Ala-bahma.

Jim Crow segregation,
Share croppin' the plantation,
Poor schools, poor education.

Rundown hood, dirt and scum,
Nothing to eat, just bread crumbs,
Spoiled milk, suck the thumb.

Eatin' salty pork rinds,
Govament cheese, welfare line,
Sippin' on a bottle of cheap wine.

A white woman hired a nanny;
She was a Black granny.
The husband grabbed her fanny.

If you really want this job
You gotta polish the knob,
Get on your knees and slob.

Grandpa beat Granny, called her a cheater;
Lost his job as a street sweeper.
He snortin' coke and smokin' reefer.

Chitty, chitty, bang, bang
Crips and Bloods street gangs
Pimps and hustlers dope slang

Inner cities full of crime,
Bullets ripping into the spine.
Caught a case, now doing time.

It's a daily attack,
Blacks still killin' Blacks.
Now they caught in the trap.

Sittin' in jail, waiting to die;
Tryna be hard, but livin' a lie.
No more tears, but I can hear the cries.

These are some of the reasons why,
But it still doesn't justify
All of this Black on Black crime.

NEEGAS CRAKKAS AND WEDBACKS

Neegas:
Got four baby mommas
Always a lot of drama
Life full of trauma
Long story with no commas

Always late
Takes his girl on a cheap date
Looking for a ten-dollar plate
Playa hate and wont congradulate

Always talkin' shit
Tryna get the fire lit
Hot wings and links on the pit
Ain't got no job cuz he quit

Momma ain't well
She livin' in hell
Daddy stuck in jail
With no bail

Kool-Aid in the pickle jar
He's a ghetto superstar
Using baby momma's EBT card
Fat rims on a busted car

Mouth rockin' gold teeth
Neck chain Jesus piece
Air Jordans on the feet
His money he can't keep

Always tryna flash
Makin' fast money cash
Smokin' a lot of grass
His girl got a fat ass

Crakkas:
Bucktooth hillbilly
Fishing in Mississippi
Always acting silly
Riding donkeys, no fillies.

Moonshine lick
Tobacco spit
Don't give a shit
Suck his sister's tit

Peeping Tom looker
Sleepin' with hookers
Always borrowing sugar
Eatin' his own boogers

Likes his eggs poached
On white bread toast
Smacking the kitchen roach
"I killed that fugger," he boast

Junkyard bash
Trailer park trash
Corned beef and hash
Always hiding the stash

In the meth lab
Bumpy skin bad
He's always mad
Cuz he lost all he had

Can't add figures
Pot belly bigger
Ready to pull the trigger
Still hanging neegers

Wedbacks:
Up all night making a plan
In the water swimming the Rio Grande
Backstroked till he hit the sand
Ducking and dodging the police man

Crossing the border is hard
Waiting to get a green card
Pulling weeds, cutting yards
Still cooking with lard

Train hoppin'
Pill poppin'
Strawberry croppin'
Fake name droppin'

Down on his luck
Tryna make a buck
Corona beer suck
Driving Taco trucks

Maria cleaning house
Stealing shit in her blouse
Homeowners think it's lost
She's illegal and cheap cost

Hiding from border patrol at night
Big families in one house tight
Beans and rice every night
Stick together ready to fight

Acting like a fool
Used as a mule
Just a small tool
Drug world rules

But you can't shut the door
Because these groups are poor
Cancel society wants to ignore
Their numbers grow more and more

BLACK LIVES MADDER

Turn on the news, it's about that time,
To see a brotha gunned down in his prime.
Police officer committed another crime,
Shooting bullets into his spine.

Body in the street, under the sunshine;
Falsify the report, police don't dime.
Blood on the hands, thick as slime;
Barely alive, wheelchair bind.

Nervous as fugg, bubble guts poot;
"Got another one", fat pig toots.
"Hands up, please don't shoot."
This time he got stomped by the boot.

Badge and gun, white man brute,
Get real mad when Black fist salute.
White supremacy is the root;
The system fuggs you like a prostitute.

He is called the Number 1 batter;
Big belly getting fatter,
Eating rib eye steak platter,
Promoted climbing the ladder.

Pull the trigger backbone shatters;
Shots rang out, the people scatter.
Shoot to kill, blood splatters;
Don't give a fugg about Black lives madder.

THE NEW CIVIL WAR

Make America Great Again
It was Tump's campaign slogan
Did politricks make him win?

Make no mistake, the hate was real;
The ugly face of racism revealed
With this Prez, Was fascism the deal?

White privileged and still mad,
Chest puffed out acting bad,
Walking around waving the American flag

Promote hate and fear was the plan;
The Neo Notzi Aryan
Wealth and dominance over the land.

Hurry up, get off the porch;
Go to the store and get a tiki torch.
Looking for a neega to scortch.

Angry white KKK,
Don't hide now, put the sheets away.
Downtown is a honky tonk parade.

The media calls them White Nationalist,
A gentle term for domestic terrorist,
Masking their hate as patriotist.

The grade school teacher,
Fire and brim stone preacher,
Turned into an evil creature.

Hillbillys with pitchforks and sticks,
Skinheads threw mortar and bricks,
None of them crakkkas can fight with fist.

Was the govament happy with this mess?
Did they want all of this civil unrest?
The people rallied to protest.

Many sides are wrong;
That was Tump's song.
He said leave the white men alone.

It's a gloomy day, no more sun;
Tap, rack and roll, grab the gun.
The new civil war has just begun.

UNITE THE FIGHT

On the freeway she was walking around,
So the police beat the sista down.

He ran towards her with a fast pace,
Savagely attacked her with blows to the face.

Big man on the block, with a side hustle,
Police surrounded him, ready to tussle.

He said he wanted no trouble today,
Killed from a chokehold, on the street he lay.

Why did he have to shoot the young man?
Trying to make sense, but can't understand.

Police said he grabbed his gun,
But really the brotha was trying to run.

He stopped in the streets with his hands up;
Shot him six times without giving a fugg.

Police, armored trucks, and riot gear,
People rallied and marched with no fear.

The racist cops were put to the test;
Now they have to deal with civil unrest.

No Messy Jessy or Sharpton in town,
Because it's time to really get down.

The people have gathered arm in arm;
They don't wanna see any more harm.

Started way back during slavery;
We were strange fruit, hanging from the tree.

Bend over, break your back in the hot sun;
Chopped your foot if you tried to run.

"He raped me!" the white hoe said;
Burn the cross at night, now the neegas dead.

Please, no more innocent bloodshed;
Nuff respect to the knotty dred.

In the 60's the Black fist was in the air;
50 years later rainbow fists are everywhere.

No need for violence and please don't loot;
We don't have to give them a reason to shoot.

Let's come together all people of color;
We don't want to bury another brotha.

So let's wake up and get in the fight;
We can win, if we unite the fight.

KAPPA NIGG

He is Colin Kappa Nigg,
Former Niner from San Francisq.
National anthem plays, he sits;
Angry fans curse and spit.

Defiant, confidant, full of swag;
Red, white, and blue flag.
The media gave him a disrespectful tag;
Ooooh!! The fake patriots are mad.

Boos rain like showers,
But Kap never cowered.
Stood tall like a tower,
Big afro, Black power.

It's about police brutality,
Black homicide casualties.
Bloody street fatalities,
Public enemy realities.

It's not about ISIS;
It's a national crisis.
By sitting he stands righteous,
Balls of steel to fight this.

Is anyone working to find a solution?
System is dirty, full of pollution.
The world is a ball of confusion;
It's all about the revolution.

Media working hard to find flaws;
Now the brotha is blackballed.
Backbone strong, he won't fall;
Kiss no ass and don't crawl.

He came to the league, real raw;
Progressed well under Har-baw.
Pocket passer? Hell naw;
New coach, last straw.

Had him on the bench;
Only played in a pinch.
Vice grip like a wrench;
You could smell the stench.

He really should start;
His talents are off the charts.
Plays with a lot of heart;
He and the league are far apart.

Full of Black pride;
Bad chick on his side.
Driving a fancy ride;
He ain't tryna hide.

Kap said, "Whatcha gonna do, suspend me
If I bend down and take a knee?"
Hell, this ain't the land of the free;
People blind to the facts, don't wanna see.

Protest the season, if you dare;
Haters mad, we don't care.
Wisdom and knowledge, we must share;
Black fist high in the air.

A BALL OF FLAMES

He brought millions of Americans joy
Eating Jell-O pudding with little girls and boys.
Gave underprivileged kids Christmas toys;
Making people laugh was his ploy.

His star was as bright as the sunshine;
He is considered one of the greatest of all time.
He stayed on TV during his prime;
Hard to believe he committed these crimes.

It's no secret, everybody knows;
This is not new, the script is old.
In Hollyweird, it's sex, drugs, and rock n roll;
Sacrifice the mind, body, and soul.

Sixty accusers sealed his fate;
Fans can't believe this all took place.
Just another tragic fall from grace;
No way Coz is guilty of rape.

He was a huge star in the 70's and 80's;
Fame and success can make you crazy.
Yes, he was married and had plenty of ladies;
He had many like Reynolds and Beatty.

They went to his place, he gave them some pills;
They claimed he assaulted them against their will.
Drugged and seduced, he was copping free feels;
He said it was consensual because they wanted Bill.

Party girls ready to meet and greet,
Offering up their goodies as a nice treat.
Hoping to hook up with a celeb in the sheets;
Bumping and grinding, out comes the freak.

Pretty young groupies looking for love,
Poppin' bottles in Heff's club.
Swingers getting tipsy in the hot tub,
Playboy bunny booty rub.

Most of these celebs did the same things;
There was no love, just one-night flings.
Little did he know what this lifestyle would bring;
A Black man in their world must kiss the ring.

White folks loved him, gave him a pass;
Elite Black man in the Boo-lay class.
He hung out with Heff listening to jazz;
These two guys have seen plenty of ass.

He was a role model to Blacks and minorities;
Lectured students from many diversities.
Gave scholarships and supported fraternities;
Contributed millions to Black universities.

He was the friendly knee grow;
He rarely cursed during his shows.
Unlike the Human Tornado,
Blaxploitation beard and afro.

In the early 90's, the shit got real;
His only son was targeted and killed.
This was devastating to Bill and wife Kamille,
Heartbreaking pain that no parent wants to feel.

He once had the Number 1 show on TV,
So he decided to buy N-Bee See.
Did this move piss off whitey?
They shot it down and denied him.

They let him know, you may be large,
But we are still in charge.
Stay in yo lane and drive your own car;
You are trying to take this too far.

The allegations came down on his bald dome;
His position in the big house was no longer strong.
He began to lose his seat next to the throne;
He was arrested and removed from his home.

Set him free, his fans signed the petition;
Pennsylvania's court overturned the conviction.
Returning to the stage was his mission;
Time to reform the criminal justice system.

Some say he is tarnished in the Hall of Shame;
His reputation destroyed in a ball of flames.
The Mee Two movement said he is to blame;
Sad story 'bout a life that won't be the same.

RIP NIP THE CRIP

Crenshaw and Slauson on the block
Hustlin t-shirts, weed, and socks
No powder, just crack rocks
Supply and demand, plenty of stock
Pistol grip on the Glock
Steady traffic, cars flock

Street code, no snitches
Move weight, collect riches
Smooth connect, no glitches
Run yo mouth and get stitches
Dead homies lay in ditches
Always money over bitches

Rapping with a gangsta flow
Skinny frame with big muscle
Never afraid to scrap or tussle
Stayed ten toes down fuh-sho
B ball love from Curry and Russell
Nipsey was known for his hussle

He owned his music masters
His pockets were getting fatter
Jealous homies getting madder
Crabs in a barrel pulling the ladder
Neglected kids getting badder
Black on Black crimes sadder

He was gonna meet with police
To promote unity and peace
To help maintain safer streets
Encourage gangs to put down the heat
He was generous to the homeless he would meet
He was into Sebi's herbs and healthy eats

Nip was not in the moody
To join the club and give up booty
Hollywould full of tooty fruity
He was a playa and had a lot of cuties
Fox motel on Western is snooty
Reppin the hood was his duty

Last time that I checked
Brothas and sistas we must protect
When you help your people you're a threat
The corrupt system will come for your neck
They don't want a positive effect
Love and unity our problems correct

He was gangbanging no more
The brotha was shot in front of his store
Assassinated Nip and ran away from the door
His death shook the hood to its core
His fans cried, tears poured
A shrine of burning candles on the floor

He was about to be bigga
He was with rogg nation and jeega
He was no ass kissa
Did somebody pay a neega
To pull the trigga
Undercover hit? Go figga

The Staple Center crowd was plenty
Respect and admiration from many
Mourners gathered in love and unity
He was proud of his culture and identity
The black hearse rolled through the community
His girl Lauren was his affinity

A powerful message from Farrakhan
Led by the Nation of Islam
Big crowds remained calm
No guns, no shots, no bombs
You could feel the neighborhood bond
Everyone continued the marathon

He made a major lifestyle transition
Uplifting the community was his ambition
Business moves and acquisitions
Entrepreneurial positions
Used his platform to improve conditions
City council Nipsey Hussle petition

Rest in peace, neighborhood Nip
Cash money flip
On the Crenshaw strip
Blue Impala dip
Yac Hennessee sip
Rollin 60 Crip

I CAN'T BREATHE

The cops were called on Big George
For an alleged twenty-dollar forge;
He was handcuffed in front of the store.

Unnecessary force and thrown on the ground;
Bystanders stunned by Floyd's anguished sounds.
Minneapolis P.D. pinned him down.

"I can't breathe," George Floyd said.
"I can't breathe," George Floyd pled.
"I can't breathe," George Floyd bled.

The racist cops ignored his cries,
Shunned the crowd as they asked why.
"Don't kill the man, don't take his life."

"Gah damn! Come on, bruh!
"Get off his neck, let him up!"
But the bitch ass pig didn't give a fugg.

The crowd recorded all of this drama,
Watching in horror the brutality and trauma,
As Floyd cried out for his deceased momma.

"I can't breathe," George Floyd said.
"I can't breathe," George Floyd pled.
"I can't breathe," George Floyd bled.

Cries fell on deaf ears and there was no hope;
The killer cop ignored all who spoke,
Hands in his pockets, applying a knee blood choke.

No more movement from Floyd's head;
"That's fugged up!" the crowd said.
No longer conscious, George Floyd was dead.

Another dead Black man for the world to see,
Another senseless murder by the police,
Another lifeless body dead in the streets.

"Black lives madder!" was shouted in the streets,
With big signs saying, "No justice, no peace,"
Rallying together, barking at the police.

Has the energy really shifted
To combat racism that's always existed?
Are we really coming together to fight this?

Defiant expressions
Toward unprovoked aggression
Against systemic oppression

Searching for clarity
And true solidarity
Without fake celebrity

Diverse crowds started peaceful protest;
Undercover racist started civil unrest,
Igniting riots, putting police to the test.

Breaking glass, looting stores;
Grabbing clothes, jewelry, and more.
Here comes the cops, run out the door.

Black mayors and Black police chiefs
Put before cameras, crying for peace,
Promoted to uphold white supremacy.

America is called "Home of the Brave,"
Built from the blood, sweat, and tears of slaves,
Wealth created for racist whites to get paid.

Racial tensions increased with Tump;
Hateful narratives woke up the bums.
His followers are the rich, poor, and dumb.

National Guards, armored gear,
Martial law to strike fear,
Curfew enforced; streets are clear.

Yes, we know the system is flawed,
But police are paid to uphold the law.
A cold-blooded murder is what we saw.

Police are now taking a knee,
Prompted by protestors who seek peace,
A token display of unity.

All officers involved, they must convict,
If not, there will be more violence,
And true peace and unity will not exist.

SELL ME A RIVER

Evacuate now, it's time to flee;
Grab your belongings, most you can't keep.
Muddy rivers roar down the street.

Hurricane Harvey on the Gulf coast,
No mo butter for the Texas toast.
Flooding waters hit Houston the most.

Church closed the door. Where is the pastor?
Quakes and hurricanes are coming faster.
Are all of them really natural disasters?

Blow up a raft for the raging river;
Float to the church for a chicken dinner.
Pay your tithes, be a cheerful giver.

Shutter all windows and block all doors;
Gas up the car, go to the store.
The big storm is coming off shore.

Irma was a bitch and couldn't be tamed;
She was the mother of all hurricanes.
Florida and the Caribbean won't be the same.

Big rumble housequake,
Glasses tumble, walls break.
Run for cover it's an earthquake.

Had the American dreama,
Big house and a new Beema,
Now beggin' for help from FEMA.

Donate, donate, donate;
Pass around the collection plate.
A lot of dirty hands are in on the take.

Who is the boss
Running the Redd Kross?
Does the money get lost?

Damp, humid, wet, and hot,
In the shelter sleeping on a cot.
Clothes in a sack is all you got.

No love for the lost in the Bible belt;
P.R. stunt, but really no help.
Greedy blood suckas look out for self.

Some call it climate gentrification,
Geo engineered to cleanse the nation,
Designed to wipe out the poor population.

No, this is real, it can't be fake;
The Bible says we in the last days.
Don't believe conspiracies, some say

This is a game that they play;
Bow your head, meditate, and pray.
The good Lord will make it safe someday.

PIMPIN' IN THE PULPIT

The longest running scam
Was the Rev Billy "Cramm."
Had all the stadiums jammed;
Paid big bucks to hear the man.

Stone cold heart breakers,
Big money makers,
All time fakers,
Jim and Tammy "Flaker."

Sweating hard T.D. "Snakes,"
Big money he rakes.
He pulls no brakes;
He in on the take.

Acted like King Kong,
Pimp hand was strong.
What he did was wrong;
Long Stroke Eddie is gone.

Everybody holla,
New jet baller,
Bible scholar
Cref "Mo" Dollar.

Top of the church is a giant cross;
Doors wide open to save the lost.
First lady of the church tryna floss;
The house is packed, new members sought.

The wrist is shiny, with all the bling;
Fingers covered with diamond rings.
Clapping his hands as the choir sings;
Congregation listens, to his words they cling.

Sunday school teaching,
Atlanta, Georgia peaching,
Fire and brimstone preaching,
Everyone he reaching.

In the parking lot sits an expensive car;
Everybody knows the owner is the star.
Mistress in the front row, legs apart;
Rev in the pulpit spittin' bars.

"Hurry up, don't be late;
Write big checks for the collection plate.
If you don't, hell is your fate;
The world needs love, stop with the hate."

"Put some cheese on that baloney;
Ain't a damn thing funny.
It's all about the money
In the land of milk and honey."

A sista called him in the middle of the night;
She was upset and very uptight.
When the preacher arrived, her dress was real tight;
She invited him in, but something wasn't right.

The house was hot, he loosened his tie;
She offered him coffee and a slice of pie.
Her husband left her, she began to cry;
Preacher laid hands on her brown thick thighs.

She pulled him close and he didn't resist;
Hot and heated, he stared at her tits.
Finally he said, "We can't do this!
"Let's get on our knees to pray and repent."

"So don't weep, dry your eyes;
Don't forget to pay your tithes.
It's all about the pie in the sky;
Come to church, you'll be all right."

Lil' old man with the crippled leg
Fell out of his wheelchair and bumped his head.
"Get up, you are healed," the pastor said;
"I perform miracles, eat this fish and bread."

Lead singer in the choir is a tenor;
Now he's saved, but he's still a sinner.
Big donations, a cheerful giver,
He is blessed with a fried chicken dinner.

Poor folks can't get a break;
Eating beans with no steak.
Bottom of the pot they scrape;
Need money for the collection plate.

So who do you blame?
Faithful members caught up in this game.
Big time preachers who flaunt their fame;
Taking advantage of the weak is a shame.

FIELD SERVICE

Turn off the water hose, here they come;
Get off the porch, in the house people run.
Briefcase and suits, you must shun;
Stop playin', can't have no fun.

My momma said she ain't at home;
The children pretended to be all alone.
But you can hear her talking on the phone;
It gets real quiet, acting like they're gone.

All of a sudden a big dog barks,
Charging fast from the back yard.
Getting out of the gate is gonna be hard,
But they made it safely back to the car.

The next day was a different case;
The man said a witness violated his space.
Yelled loud and slammed the door in his face;
Head held high, he was not disgraced.

She answered the door in a night gown;
Big breast, small waist, and her hips were round.
She invited him in to stick around;
Very tempting, but he had to bounce.

The house on the corner with all of the cats,
Trash everywhere and it stinks very bad;
Looks like a hoarder living in this pad,
Invited them in, nervously they sat.

Strange things happen every day in the field;
Came face to face with a piece of steel.
Bible in hand serves as a shield;
Bravely press on, ministry zeal.

They called it the truth, back in the day;
Book bag full of Watchtower and Awake.
Servicing the hood in a ruff place;
No fear, stay ready, Jah made it safe.

JUS GOT PAID

Jus got paid
Barber shop fade
Suits custom made
Sharp as a blade

Gotta wear shades
My girl got braids
Perfume she sprayed
She ready to get laid

As the music played
Cards, it was spades
Basketball D Wade
The Lakers need a trade

The police made a raid
The house was section aid
Somebody got slayed
Close my eyes and prayed

People were afraid
Time to leave, I strayed
Smart in school, got grades
I jus got paid

FIRE IMPIRE

The daddy's a demon and a lion;
The momma is screaming and crying.
The sons are dreaming and fighting;
Everyone is scheming and backbiting.

A Black dysfunctional family
Was shown every week on TV
For the whole world to see,
Featuring Lushus and Cooky.

Cooky's on the rag;
Jammal is a vagg.
Hakem think he bad;
Lushus always mad.

Dre is losing his head;
Momma running from the feds.
Jammal got punks in his bed;
The lions about makin' that bread.

Network TV is all about the buck,
But I wanna know what's up
With showing Black men fugg,
Lip lock, and prick sugg.

Is men kissing men natural?
Homophobic society is factual.
Destructive consequences actual;
Programming the mind is tactical.

Well I'll be damned,
It's still the master plan
To feminize the Black man,
Break him down if you can.

A lot of strong hate,
Their will must break.
Cut the nuts, castrate,
Watch the gate, depopulate.

The message is very clear:
Make these coons queer.
They have no fear
When taking it in the rear.

Leave your wife in jail;
No visits, no bail.
When she gets out, give her hell;
Keep her under your spell.

None of them are bright;
Black family ain't tight.
Look at them neegas fight;
This shit ain't right.

The house is on fire;
The devil is a liar.
To all viewers and buyers,
Fire Impire.

CRACKATOSIS HYPNOSIS

Don't rock the boat, can't spill the money;
Addressing issues, no way, no dummy.
Life is good, Malibu Beach sunny;
Living large in the land of milk and honey.

Far removed from canned fish and crackers,
Black celebs feast on high end platters.
Some even support Black Lives Madder;
When the streets get muddy, to the hills they scatter.

Black man sold his soul to the game;
Many shows on TV, please explain.
Is Heev Starvy kissin' ass with no shame?
Is he the new conductor on the coon train?

Light skinned sista got a pass,
Conservative puppet for the right-wing class.
Pandering statements ended her career fast;
Bye, bye pretty face Stacy Crash.

Big, black, bold, and round,
Charlz Barkee got a lot of rebounds.
Another basketball analyst clown
Agreed with verdict when Trayvon was gunned down.

Amer-I-Kan man of renown
Gained famed for scoring touchdowns.
Was an actor and activist with boots on the ground;
I can't believe they flipped Gym Brown.

Jesus walks, the choir rejoiced;
Yay tried to be Black community's voice.
Neega told the world slavery was a choice,
Dropped out of college, from Illinois.

Tyger was trained by his daddy, Earl;
He became the best golfer in the world.
He was on top, down with the swirl;
Swinging his club deep inside white girls.

He made it big as a Prince in Bell Air;
Sixx degrees of separation, his ass was bare.
Bent for Hollywould, ready to share;
Thrill Smiff is a star with plenty flare.

Started with Shammy Davis Jr and his crew,
The Ratt Pac, the Mobb, and a Black few.
This nigga was rich wearing a pompadour do;
Buck dancing for trinkets with a soft tap shoe.

America loved him and called him the Juice;
Accused of killing his ex and some white dude.
The famous car chase was all on the news;
Not guilty? Got busted, now O-Jay is loose.

Ballers wear his shoes to walk around;
He is no king, but he still wears the crown.
Air Jourdin soared above the clouds;
He's quiet on Black issues, won't say nothing, wow!

Now I lay me down to sleep;
A glass of milk and Oreos please.
Chocolate cookies with white cream;
Neegas knocked out with crackatosis dreams.

STOP BLACK DESTRUCTION

Colonialism on the African continent,
Established to show white power and dominance.

Economic rape of mother Africa,
Starvation swole, smile for the camera.

Disease the African and Caribbean for experimentation,
Designed by world's elite to reduce Black population.

It's the destruction of African civilization,
Famine, wars, destabilization.

Independent African leader assassination,
Worldwide media spread misinformation

Stolen and buried African history and artifacts,
Sitting in European museums and not giving it back.

Eliminate African culture from American Black people;
Keep them intoxicated, feed grass to the sheeple.

Divide Black people based on skin color;
Teach them to not trust but hate each other.

Make them dependent on welfare,
Poor education, and inadequate health care.

Poor housing and ghetto slums,
Homeless addicts living as bums.

Unemployment always high,
Contributes to theft and rising crime.

Lynching and castration of Black people,
Demonic forces, pure evil.

Corrupt laws enforced to steal Black land,
Torched Black towns by mobs of white men.

Brainwashed to worship a pale Jesus Christ,
Black slaves crucified a sacrificial life.

Black men depicted as animals and savages,
Survived deathly slave ships during the middle passage.

Black female sexual exploitation,
Humiliated and molested by perverted Caucasians.

We can stop all of this Black destruction;
No elections, armed protection to start an eruption.

Shake off the concussion;
Have less discussion.

Listen to intelligent instruction;
Hear the African drum percussion.

WAKE UP, MY BROTHA

Shackles on the brain, you are no threat;
Locked into a plantation mindset,
Skeptical if you learn a new concept.

Constipated mind, full of shitty thoughts,
Incapable of thinking beyond what was taught.
Institutional achievements, but manhood is sought.

Just a dumb ass gee
With a college degree,
Emancipated, but still not free.

They give you a job, if you call 'em "boss,"
Brown nose kiss ass, self-respect is lost.
Coonin ass knee grows come with a cost.

Red, white, and blue, home of the brave;
Act right, boy, learn to behave.
Still a servant, but not a slave.

The servant and slave do not belong to themselves;
They are owned and controlled by someone else.
Learn your culture, identify yourself.

Don't call your queen a hoe or a bitch;
Her ass you don't kick, so put down your fist.
Love her, lead her, learn to get rich.

Don't spend all day laying in the sack,
Beatin up her pussy and blowin' out her back.
Develop a think tank and go earn your stacks.

Open your mind, begin to read,
Share all of your knowledge, give to your seed.
Young kings and queens we must breed.

The system we live in is full of deceit;
Schools full of miseducation they teach.
Can of bullshit, packaged nice and neat.

Don't be deceived by Uncle Sam;
Stand up, be strong, African man.
Do this and you spoil the racist plan.

Be sound in mind, body, and soul;
It takes courage to be brave and bold,
Because we have a story that must be told.

Wait, hold up, let's all stand up;
Can't stay down, we must get up.
It's time to mentally and physically wake up!!

www.ingramcontent.com/pod-product-compliance
Lightning Source LLC
LaVergne TN
LVHW091556060526
838200LV00036B/865